For my beautiful wife, Anita-Clare, about
whom many of these poems are written

Published by The Samphire Publishing
Company
94 Westwood Hill
London
SE26 6PD

ISBN; 978-0-993515-0 1

A FOUR-LETTER WORD

CARO NESS

This volume of my poetry is devoted to love. Love comes in many guises, from the love we have for a partner or parent, to the love we feel for our child. Or it may be the love we feel for a pet, or an animal's love for its owner or another animal. I make no bones about having a sweet tooth, so it may even be an overwhelming love for sweets or cake! Love can be pyrotechnical and urgent or something steadfast, quiet and strong. To love or be loved transforms us.

The poem on page 6, for example, recounts the extraordinary events that occurred on the night my mother died. She loved owls and they came in droves to sit on the roof of the house and the surrounding farm buildings, hooting loudly. It was as if they had come to call her home.

As John Lennon so rightly wrote:

"And in the end, the love you take, is equal to the love you make."

CONTENTS

OUR MOTHER'S GOODBYE

Owls held a special significance
For our mother.
She loved the barn owls that lived
In the buildings round our house,
The screech owls that called
From the lime trees,
The little owls that clung tenaciously
To the phone wires.
Just before she died
The owls started hooting.
They came from everywhere,
Many of them,
Calling her home.
And since then,
People we know have commented,
"What is it with the owls?
They're calling more often
And at unusual times during the day."
And we, her family,
Have noticed, in turn,
That it is always those friends
Our mother did not have the chance
To say goodbye to
Before she died.

A FOUR-LETTER WORD

Love is just a four-letter word

Like long, or like, or wish, or hope,

Yet, though it may seem quite absurd,

It encircles the heart with silken rope,

And makes each day seem bright and new,

With myriad wonderful things to do.

No hill too steep, no road too far,

To be precisely where YOU are!

You, the lover, you the muse,

You the beautiful dancing shoes

That sashay into the mind, the brain,

And linger, like a sweet refrain,

That needs discovering again and again....

Love is just a four-letter word,

Like sing, or grin, or feel or hold,

Yet it's the icing on the cake,

The greatest story ever told.

It's the fizz in a fine champagne,

It's the huff and puff of an old steam train

The breeze breathing gently on your face

The intricacies of a piece of lace,

It's euphoria, it's a dream

It's the cherry on top of a large ice cream,

It's a name you can't ignore

If I'm the apple, you're its core,

It's a megatastic superstore.

Love is just a four-letter word,

But oh, it is so much MORE.

I WROTE A MESSAGE IN THE SAND

I wrote a message in the sand,

I used sticks and shells,

To decorate,

Illuminate,

To make 3D.

L · O · V · E

And although we both know...

That the tide will come in,

And the waves will wash away

This gentle, personal communiqué,

We also know this,

Its sentiment will remain,

Impressed into the sand...

LOVE REMEMBERED

It was a year ago, today,

That we met on the dance floor.

Someone took a photo of us.

Two lonely people in a fluid, graceful embrace.

And yet the moment

My right hand rested in the small of your back,

And I held your hand in my left,

My world was not solitary any more,

It was peopled with you,

Just you.

THE SOUND OF YOUR LAUGHTER

I love the way you laugh.

Like a peal of hand bells

With perfect pitch.

Or the sonorous belly laugh of a wind chime.

And when you laugh until you weep,

So that fat tears, good tears,

Drench your cheeks,

And you shake uncontrollably

With the joy of it.

What about when you are faced with the ridiculous?

So that your laughs scatter

Like gunshots of rapid rifle fire?

And those low chuckles that seem to start

Somewhere near your toes?

Your laughter is medicine, a sunburst, a holiday,

Infectious, inclusive, individual,

As are you.

I just love the way you laugh.

11

YOU ARE THE ONE

Your laugh is fat and fills my soul,
The two of us giggling's a perfect whole,
For you I'd walk from pole to pole,
Because you are the one.

I go weak when I hear your voice,
Your presence makes my heart rejoice,
It's you, there is no other choice,
Because you are the one.

I sense it when you walk in a room,
Emotions well in a giant flume,
My pulse rate quickens, my heart goes boom,
Because you are the one.

I love your perfume, love your scent,
I believe you're heaven-sent,
Time with you is time well spent,
Because you are the one.

Being with you is a wonderland,
It's an adventure, and it's grand,
I'm happy to simply hold your hand,
Because you are the one.

You're my lover, you're my muse,
Each day with you's a giant schmooze,
You're my treasure, how can I lose?
Because you are the one.

WAITING

I have waited here for you.
Not long today
But this day is just one of many.

I have waited here for you
Because this spot is where
I remember you last.

I have waited here for you.
Wondering idly
If I will know you now, after all this time.

I have waited here for you.
Will I immediately feel a sense of you
The moment you walk back into my world?

I have waited here for you.

OUR SONG

You and me against the world,
Just like dormice, inter-curled,
Our store set out, our flag unfurled,
Two bodies yet one heart.

Our home is safe, our home is calm,
A never-ending source of balm,
All who enter, feel its charm,
It is a place apart.

Things are really what they seem,
We make the perfect unit, team,
We share a future, share a dream,
Two bodies yet one heart.

THIS IS HAPPY

With you I get a tingle from my head to my toes,
That out of everyone else, it's me that you chose,
That with each day that passes, my love for you grows,
This is happy.... and I like it.

You walked into my life and swept away woes,
The door to unhappiness started to close,
Our love is spiritual, both of us knows,
This is happy.... and I like it.

It's as if past misfortunes suddenly froze,
We have high after high and very few lows,
You restored trust and faith and oh, how it shows,
This is happy.... and I like it.

You're a merchant ship laden with precious cargoes,
You're a melody, poetry, my purple prose,
You're a ditty that Gershwin chose to compose,
This is happy.... and I like it.

You're the pot of gold, and the rainbows,
You're the headlining star and the sideshows,
You're a brilliant photograph about to expose,
This is happy.... and I like it.

So yes, I confess it, it's not hard to disclose,
You're my stunning white lily, my perfect red rose,
With each day that passes, my heart overflows,
This is happy.... and I like it.

YESTERDAY AND TODAY

Yesterday represents some bad times past.
Relationships I thought would last.
Times I'm told were full of fun,
But hardship outnumbered that, ten to one.

Today represents us, that's me and you,
You made everything right when it was askew.
You brought meaning to feeling so secure,
We are bound by a love enduring and mature.

Yesterday seems full of ills and woes,
Of grief, betrayal, all-time lows.
Of mental cruelty, disrespect,
Of endless attacks on soul and intellect.

Today is joyful, full of hope.
Of sun-filled days that envelope.
Surrounded by those that we adore
And promise of better things in store!

THE SWING

I love this spot

It is a place of magic

I used to come here as a child

And see how high

I could swing

The fence posts marched

Down the hill

And I would try to reach them

And on autumn days

When the leaves began to fall

It felt as if the trees themselves

Were scattering gold nuggets at my feet

SWEETS

I love a good old jelly tot,

I love a gummy bear,

I love an American hard gum,

And I've Licorice Allsorts to spare!

I only buy bags of nostalgia,

A box of traditional sweets,

I am big on the taste of the 70's,

So all the above constitute treats!

MY GRANDFATHER'S FARM

It was years since I'd visited

My grandfather's farm,

It had become inaccessible,

The grass now grew across the road,

And the fence posts clung to one another,

Drunkenly,

Connected by sad and futile bits of wire

A morning mist hovered,

Half-burned by the sun,

Which threw long shadows down the track.

It would have been sad,

But for the trees that lent their shade,

And crowded the path in a protective embrace,

Returning fond snatches of memory to me

Of my grandfather's farm.

LOVE TIPTOED IN

Love tiptoed quietly into my heart,

And planted its seed deep within.

I realised that you were a woman apart,

As you crept stealthily under my skin.

I cannot convey what I found that day,

The day that we very first met,

A meeting of minds that one rarely finds,

That I haven't recovered from yet.

You are my lover, you are my muse,

Scratch me and you will find residues,

Of you in my heart, my blood, my brain,

Traces of you will always remain...

MY MOTHER GET'S HOME

I know I'm always impatient at this time of day,

But I love it when she gets home.

I look out till I see her come around the corner,

And into our street.

The determined swing of her arms.

Her quick feet on the pavement,

The tune she hums as she walks.

She tells me it's her favourite time of day,

Her "me and you" time.

Our "us" time,

When we cook together,

Laugh together,

Tell each other about our day.

And then bed,

And a chapter of the latest book

We've chosen to read.

I love it at this time of day,

...when my mother gets home.

THE WALK

I was sad,

Sad about you and I,

We had argued,

So I took myself

For a solitary walk.

The skies seemed to

Echo my mood,

Stormy,

Angry,

Turbulent.

And then,

As I thought more

About you and I,

Clouds,

Like puffballs,

Built and massed,

And my spirits lifted

With them.

LET'S GO TO A HOTEL

I loved you madly from the first,
You give me a hunger and a thirst,
I can't get my mind off your behind,
Oh, let's go to a hotel!

I love the way your hair falls just so,
I love your energy, your get up and go,
I hear you speak and my legs go weak,
Oh, let's go to a hotel!

I intuit your presence when you walk in,
You're my guilty pleasure, my luscious sin,
I love your eyes, it's no surprise,
Oh, let's go to a hotel!

You're my touchstone, you're my muse,
I want to walk marathons in your shoes,
I hear your voice and I rejoice,
Oh, let's go to a hotel.

I cannot convey how you make me feel,
It's magical, flammable, quite surreal,
I know I'll follow wherever you go,
Oh, let's go to a hotel!

I love your touch, I love your scent,
Time with you is time well spent,
Your wizardry bewitches me,
Oh let's go to a hotel!

I love the way you laugh, you smile,
You know just how to attract, beguile,
You give me more than I could ever ask for,
Oh, let's go to a hotel!

You know that you're my first, my last,
You're my future, forget the past,
Everything true, is bound up in you,
Oh, let's go to a hotel!

SOMETHING ABOUT YOU

The way you move, the way you walk,
The way you sing, the way you talk,
There's something about you I love.

The way you laugh, to fill your boots,
The way you blush to your very roots,
There's something about you I love.

The way that you smile, with your mouth and your eyes,
The expression you make if you get a surprise,
There's something about you I love.

Your humour, both gentle and mischievous too,
Your sadness when you have to bid a friend adieu,
There's something about you I love.

Your beautiful eyes, a luminous green,
Your cooking at which you are undoubtedly queen,
There's something about you I love.

You make me feel cherished, make me feel loved,
For your tenderness, kindness and all the above,
There's something about you I love.

LOVE'S GREAT ADVENTURE

You cannot be happy without having felt pain,

You need to hit rock bottom before you surface again.

You cannot be loving unless you understand,

What it is to be giving, to provide with both hands.

Love's an adventure, it's also a gift,

It's like finding the shore when you've been set adrift.

It's a firework, or Christmas, or the 4th of July,

It makes you believe you can reach for the sky.

There are no limits, no boundaries in sight,

Love gives you courage, buckle up and take flight.

A QUESTION OF BELONGING

What makes my heart beat fast, so fast?

What makes me weak at the knees?

Your scent intoxicates and lasts,

You invade me like a luscious sneeze.

Stand near and my heart jumps in my chest,

Hold me close and I'm aflame,

I'm a junkie, self-professed,

I just love your voice, your name.

You're my music, softly played,

You're my lyric, you're my song,

In the full sun, you're my shade,

It's to you that I belong.

THE PLEDGE

I give you this pledge,

That I'll always be there.

To support you, protect you,

To show you I care.

You are my touchstone,

You are my world,

You walked into my life,

And I kind of unfurled.

You're laughter, you're humour,

You're a centre of joy,

You're a bundle of energy,

Just point and deploy!

There's nothing on earth,

That I wouldn't do,

To show you precisely

How much I love you.

BE BRAVE

You've been out in the wasteland,

But nirvana's close at hand,

You have a choice,

So raise your voice,

The world's at your command.

I know it won't be easy,

Events are never planned,

You have a place,

So just have faith,

Go on, take your stand.

You know you have a talent,

For putting others at their ease,

A skill at people management,

That you make look like a breeze.

Your head is full of plans and schemes,

Of comfort food and panaceas,

These are not idle, foolish dreams,

But myriad, great ideas.

So set your shoulders four square,

And step into the light.

There's nothing that you cannot dare,

Your future's clear and bright.

CROWCOMBE GATE

Across the cattle grid and wind uphill,

Through ancient, twisting burr oak trees,

That unfurl above your head until

You reach the gorse and honey bees.

Here the heather starts to grow

In patches on the open moor,

Amidst ivy, balls of mistletoe,

And pine cones strewn on forest floor.

Wild ponies graze here, shy and quick

To move away from passers-by,

The woods are lush and they are thick,

So dense you cannot see the sky.

Ancient paths carve through this place,

Tracks that somehow man forgot,

You sense a timelessness and space,

Leading to some unknown spot.

Slopes drop very steeply down

Into a sparkling cobalt sea,

And high up there upon the crown

Of land, buzzards spiral lazily.

From here on sun-drenched summer days,

A real tranquility prevails,

And if not for a smoky haze,

You'd see clear across to Wales.

This place is beauty at its best,

This is truly god's own land,

This is calm and peace expressed

By Nature's loving hand.

A IS FOR ANITA

A's for amour, for passion, for love,

As when my hand fits yours like a comfortable glove.

A's for affection, for instant rapport,

For that fatal attraction, well you know the score.

A's for the ambition to be by your side,

We are open and honest, there's nothing to hide.

A's for arrival, the moment we met,

A bolt from the blue I've not recovered from yet.

A's for Anita, the love of my life,

My soulmate, my succour, my lover, my wife.

THE EYES SAY IT ALL

In your eyes,

I am ten feet tall,

There's nothing I can't do at all.

In your eyes,

I'm a heroine,

A Stradivarius violin.

In your eyes,

I do no wrong,

I'm an Oscar-winning song.

In my eyes,

You see reflections of

A selfless, mindful, heart-felt love.

Your eyes are

Windows to your soul,

A stunning, wondrous, precious whole

THE VIGIL

Every day, you'll find me in this spot,

Staring out to sea, as like as not,

Waiting for my love to return to me,

From weeks, or months, out on the sea.

I check the wind, the swell, the tides,

And ever so much more besides,

I want to welcome home my galley cat,

The feline on the 'Tit For Tat'.

SWEETHEARTS

I was 18 when I met you,

And you were 22,

I loved your sense of humour,

And those stunning eyes of blue.

We waited to get married,

Until I was 21,

But spent each day together,

Surprising everyone.

And now we celebrate our grandchild,

Whose wedding is today,

And we could make our vows again,

Because our feelings still hold sway.

I'm now an ancient 88,

And you are 92,

But I may as well be in my teens,

Because, darling, I love you.

CAKE

I don't mind saying, there's no mistake,

I am a big fan of a birthday cake!

I'm really happy as a clam,

With a Victoria sandwich with oodles of jam!

Or a really lovely chocolate sponge,

So I can cover my face with cream and grunge!

So don't hold back! Just load my plate,

I've an empty stomach, my need is great!

WHAT LOVE IS

When I think about what love is

My heart turns over, my blood starts to fizz.

When I am asked what love represents,

I say it takes over in every sense.

So what exactly is it that love involves?

It's someone around whom your world revolves.

It's someone who makes you feel safe and warm,

Protected and sheltered, a port in a storm.

I love your eyes, I love your skin,

Where your body ends, there I begin.

YOU

I've walked the universe you to find,

Look back and I am right behind.

There for comfort and support,

To anticipate your every thought.

You're my backbone, I'll be yours,

To help you settle any scores,

I'd walk through fire to set you free,

To show you what you mean to me.

There's nothing that I wouldn't do,

To let your talents shine on through.

You are thoughtful, loving, kind,

A gem like you is hard to find.

I know my faults and there are many,

But in you I just cannot find any.

You are so brilliant yet insecure,

So darling I want to make you sure,

Sure I'll be here, right by your side,

To support you through a bumpy ride,

But also to share your triumphs too,

Because, my darling, I love you.

SAYING FAREWELL TO MY CHILD

If conversation starts to pall
And I have no words at all
Don't criticise for hating sad goodbyes,
I'm saying farewell to my child

I've always encouraged independence of thought
That luxury is so dearly sought
I need to know you have space to grow
But I'm saying farewell to my child

I want you to flourish, I want you to fly,
Don't want you to see heartache, to see me cry
Don't want to hold you back, but it's courage I lack
When I'm saying farewell to my child

I love that you engage with young and old
That your social ease makes you seem quite bold
But I sometimes love to be the hand that you hold
I don't want to say farewell to my child

You're making all kinds of exciting plans
Travelling to far-off distant lands
Though I wish you well, I think you can tell
I hate saying farewell to my child

TRUE LOVE

I fell in love with you

At the very first glimpse

You were quicksilver

Poetry in motion

A Jack in the box

My exact, male counterpart

I remember you saying

You wanted to still

Be holding my hand at 90

And here we are

60 years married

And still walking like a couple

Newly in love

A CHILD OF LIGHT

I felt you,

Felt you growing inside me.

The whisper of your movement

The percussion of your heartbeat

The sharp stab of a foot or arm

Adjusting to limited space.

I dreamed of you.

And one day,

There you were,

Fully formed,

Beautiful.

No time for a water birth

You rocketed into the world

Like a shooting star.

When you took your first breath,

I swear you smiled.

And priceless as you are,

You've been a

Child of light

Ever since.

JOURNEY

How do I know when I meet someone,
That my exquisite journey has just begun,
That there's no one on earth or under the sun,
Who makes me feel so complete.?

How do I test my intuition,
That has placed me in this extraordinarily great position,
That this is a match made in heaven, no war of attrition,
And this woman makes me feel replete?

How do I put one foot in front of another,
How do I suppress the urge to fuss or smother,
Because I know there is simply no other,
Who makes me feel so grand and upbeat?

How do I resist the need to feel,
That my world without her is sad and surreal,
That there's just one more moment I'd gladly steal,
And run the risk of being indiscreet!

It's with you I want to spend every day,
Showing you in every possible way,
That our love is large and it's here to stay,
That in us, two halves of a whole simply meet.

THE ROAD WELL-TRAVELLED

This road is so well-travelled,

Each wooden batten known,

Each bush along its borders,

Marks the time that's flown.

I recognise the mist that lingers,

That spreads across the forest floor,

I know its chilly fingers,

That grip from times before.

I know this road well-travelled,

The land it passes through,

Above all, I know each twist and turn,

Because this path leads to you...

IF MY LOVE

If my love were like an ocean,
It would come in but never retreat.
I would show you my constant devotion,
By laying it here, at your feet.

If my love were like a mountain,
It would be a peak I longed to climb,
It would bathe you like a fountain,
And stand the test of time.

If my love were like a river, long,
It would flow joyfully from its source,
It would be, like a melody or song,
Full of vigour, life and force.

If my love were like a giant oak,
It would spread its branches wide,
To shelter you and to invoke
A safe haven in which to reside.

If my love were like a garden,
You'd know it's where you belong,
It would be your own sweet Arden,
Filled with music, laughter, song.

A FELINE LOVE AFFAIR

We're two gingernuts, who, against the odds,

Outwitted our owners, the skanky sods!

Paprika's tried to lock her away,

To "keep her apart from that nasty stray."

But I'll have you know, Mr. Robert Paul,

My forebears are gentlemen, one and all!

I am no average, standard mog,

I'm digital, not analogue!

You will not part us, our love is strong,

It's to each other that we belong.

I'll climb up to your boudoir, like Romeo,

To prove I'm no worthless lothario!

We will be together, through thick and thin,

You're Elsa to my Lohengrin!

I am currently author of Caro Ness Author, a collection of poetry and prose and co-publisher of a highly successful food blog, Lover of Creating Flavours and alongside my wife run the hugely popular and well-received micro bistro La Petite Bouchee. Formerly, I have been a freelance editor, working for most of the London publishers, author and author's agent. I was Senior Commissioning Editor and formerly Managing Editor, Illustrated Division, Element Books. I was a freelance editorial, contracts and rights consultant. Commissioning Editor and Rights Manager, Liber Press. I did Maternity leave cover for the Rights Director, Virago Press. I spent 7 years with a leading literary agency dealing in fiction and non-fiction, representing the likes of Roald Dahl, Penelope Lively, J.M. Coetzee, Michael Morpurgo, Dame Jacqueline Wilson and Anne Fine. I have written 4 children's books, one of which won an award in the US, have translated one and have written three adult non-fiction titles, two for Dorling Kindersley and one for Frances Lincoln and Tuttle, USA. My books are published in 23 countries.

Printed in Great Britain
By Amazon.co.uk.Ltd.
Marston Gate